A VERY NECESSARY WINE JOKE BOOK

Plus Jokes About Husbands, Dating, Dieting, Men, the Gym and Life!

Zack Halliday

To_____

From_____

Welcome to 'A Very Necessary Wine Joke Book.' **Full of new jokes for 2022.**

We wrote the book for you to enjoy or to give as a great gift for friends or family members. Use the paperback as a present or stocking stuffer. Or send the Kindle version (to be read on their phone, tablet or laptop,) as an online present or as a last minute gift!

With this book laughs are guaranteed!

We hope you enjoy. If you do, please tell others about our book and leave us a positive review with Amazon and perhaps a high star rating.... It is really important to us and we would greatly appreciated it.

Thank you. Zack Halliday

~ **Somewhere in the world it's wine-thirty!**

~ I am so tired of my friends who cannot handle their wine. **Last night they dropped me three times carrying**

me to the car.

~ Let's drink some wine.
**It's not good to keep
things bottled up.**

~ Is it okay to pull the bag
of wine out of the box and
stab a straw into it like it's
a giant adult Capri Sun?
Asking for a friend.

~ I tried cooking with wine.
**It didn't go well, after 5 glasses I
forgot why I was in the kitchen.**

~ I enjoy long romantic walks **down the wine aisle.**

~ A friend texted me: Let's meet up for coffee this week. **Me: You spelled wine wrong.**

~ Find out how loud your partner can scream by waking them up on a plane flight **while wearing your life jacket and oxygen mask!**

~ Anyone who doesn't know what to buy me for Christmas, **clearly doesn't know where to buy wine.**

Me: "I'm still tired from all the CrossFit this morning."

Friend: "It's pronounced 'croissant' and you ate four of them."

~ Wine: *Noun.*
An alcoholic drink that is made
from fermented grapes and
therefore it officially counts
as a serving of salad.

~ This, Ma'am, is our
'Thanksgiving' Cabernet,
**it goes well with turkey
and difficult relatives.**

~ Part of me says I should
slow down on the drinking.
**The other part says,
'Don't listen to her, she's drunk.'**

~ I got a phone call while I was in the wine bar, "If you don't get home in ten minutes I'm giving your dinner to the dog." **So I went home, I love that dog.**

~ Imagine, if you will, a world in which Youtube, Twitter and Facebook **merge to become known as YouTwitFace.**

~ Every New Year's Eve I tell myself, "Deborah, next year you're gonna stay away from wine!" **Luckily my name isn't Deborah!**

~ Wine is the most nutritional beverage on the planet. It also makes you more attractive to the opposite sex, smarter and funnier. **Oh, and makes you a kickass dancer!**

'It's not how many times you fall.' I said, proudly. 'It's about how many times you get back up.'

The cop replied, 'Ma'am, that's not how sobriety tests work.'

~ Me: How much is the rent for this amazing apartment?
Him: **Ma'am, this is the supermarket wine aisle.**

~ Me: Alexa, remind me to go to the gym today.
Alexa: I have added gin to your shopping list.
Me: Close enough.

~ I'm saving this bottle of wine for a rainy day.
Oh, what the hell, it must be raining somewhere.

~ Men are like wine - they start out like grapes and it's our job to stomp on them a bit and keep them in the dark. **Till they mature into something you'd like to have dinner with.**

~ Does anyone know where adults can go trick or treating? Looking for a neighborhood that hands out Tacos and Margaritas? **Asking for a friend.**

~ Wine must only be

consumed on days of the week **with an 'a' in them.**

My horoscope says I will meet the man of my dreams today.

Not sure how my husband will take the news, but I'm pretty damn excited.

~ I drink wine because I don't like to keep things bottled up.

~ Money can't buy happiness. Just kidding, yes it can, **if that money is used to buy wine.**

Carol decided to follow her friend's advice
and not keep things bottled up.

~ I drink one glass of wine each
night for its health benefits.
**The other glasses are for
my witty comebacks and**

flawless dance moves.

~ Overheard: "Kids are challenging, **wine is necessary.**"

~ Very proud of myself, today I made a fruit salad. I started with a slice of lime, added half a strawberry, **and then tossed them with some gin and tonic.**

~ I have a bumper sticker that says, 'Honk if you think I'm good-looking and sexy.'

Then I just sit at green lights until I feel better about myself.

~ Of course size matters, **nobody wants a small glass of wine.**

~ I can't believe how strong the winds were last night…. **I only nipped out to get some milk and, somehow, I got blown into a wine bar.**

~ Wine: **It maintains my sunny personality.**

~ Why wine?
**Cause no great story ever
started with someone
eating a salad.**

~ Parenting is buying a bounce-house and swing-set just so you can sit on the patio and drink wine in peace.

~ Wine: Now cheaper than gas. **Drink, don't drive.**

~ Me, sobbing my heart out, eyes swollen, nose red: 'I can't see you anymore - I am not going to let you hurt me like this again!' **Trainer: "It was one sit up. You did one sit up."**

~ To me the term 'drink responsibly' means, **don't spill any.**

~ In a recent survey, oak trees said they don't mind being chopped down, as **long as they are made into barrels and filled with wine.**

So, I can't bring a stick inside

But you're allowed a whole tree?

~ What's the difference between a glass of wine and a man?
A glass of wine hits the spot every time.

~ I can't really walk the
walk or talk the talk.
**But if you need somebody to
drink the drinks, I'm all yours!**

~ A woman's place is
in the kitchen.
**Sitting with her feet
up, drinking a glass of
wine while watching her
husband cook dinner.**

~ Some things are better
left unsaid, but I'll probably
drink some wine
and say them anyway.

~ This girl was going on and on about making ice cubes out of left-over wine. **I was confused, what is leftover wine?**

~ Do you know what's fun about being sober? **Nothing!**

~ I'm a wine enthusiast. The more I drink, **the more enthusiastic I become!**

~ There should always be

a bottle of sparkling wine
in your fridge. Always.
Don't question it. Just do it!

~ Vodka vs Wine:

A person with a basement
full of vodka = Alcoholic!
**A person with a basement
full of wine = Classy!**

~ I am an official wine
taster. **Just buy me wine
and I'll taste it.**

~ It's Wednesday, hang in there!
Love,
Wine.

~ Marriage is just a nice word for
adopting a fully grown man

who can't take care of himself.

~ Winetaster: **Will work for free!**

Him: "Why did you marry me?"

Me: "Because you're funny."

Him: "I thought it was because
I was smart and a good lover?"

Me: "There. You see. You're
hilarious."

~ He asked me how I
get it all done…
Coffee and wine, sweetheart.
Coffee and wine.

~ Some people say that laughter
is the best medicine.
But I think a bottle of
wine is the way to go.

Sleeping next to someone you love

makes you fall asleep faster, reduces depression, and helps you live longer.

UNTIL THEY START TO SNORE

~ Tonge twister of the day:
How much whine would a wine-drinker whine if a wine-drinker couldn't drink wine?

~ I'm going to write 'drink wine' on my to-do list, **just so I can feel like I accomplished something.**

~ There are two types of people in the world. **People you want to drink with and people who make you want to drink!**

~ Dear mother-in-law, stop telling me how to raise my kids. **I live with one of yours and I've seen your work.**

Who called you a bad dog? Point them out. I will end them...

~ The more wine I drink
the better I get at
**pronouncing the name of
the wine I'm drinking.**

~ The difference between a glass
of wine and your opinion,
**is that I asked for a
glass of wine.**

~ Got my first date of the
year lined up. It's a court
date but, hey, **it's still a date
and I'm dressing up.**

~ I'm the outdoorsy type,

I drink my wine on the patio.

WHEN YOU THOUGHT YOU WERE DONE ARGUING WITH YOUR MAN

BUT THEN YOU HEAR HIM MUMBLE SOMETHING UNDER HIS BREATH

~ Unlike milk,
it's okay to cry over spilt wine.

~ Workout tip: **Get really
heavy wine glasses.**

~ I'm passing this on because it
worked for me. My doctor said
that in order to have inner peace
we should always finish things
we start. So, I looked round the
house today to find things I've
started and haven't finished.
I finished a bottle of Merlot,
a bottle of Chardonnay,
a bodle of Baileys, a butle

of wum, the remainder of
Valiuminun pisscriptins
and a box of choclutz.
Yu has no idr how fablus I
feel rite now. Sned this to all
ur frenz who need inner piss.
Oh, an telum I luvum.

~ Whisper me those three
little words every woman

wants to hear:
Him: "I brought wine."

~ It's not that I was against
working-out or running.
But I kept spilling my wine.

~ I just fired myself from
cleaning my house.
**Two reasons, I needed a drink
and I don't like my attitude.**

~ My husband stopped
and said, "You're not even
listening, are you?"
I thought that's a pretty weird

way to start a conversation.

~ Some people need a special occasion to enjoy a little wine. **I just need a glass.**

~ I have not figured out how to have a wine collection... **I do however have an extensive cork collection.**

If I'm reading the instructions correctly, after 3 glasses of wine the bookshelf assembles itself.

~ I said I'd have 2 glasses of wine and be home by 10.
I always get those two

numbers mixed up.

~ A mother's sacrifice isn't
just giving birth.
**It's also nine months
without wine.**

~ I went for a run today. It was a
wine run, but I broke a sweat.
I believe that counts.

~ There are days when you
need a second glass of wine.
**And then there are days when
you need that second bottle.**

~ Every McDonald's should have a flag they fly at half-mast **when the ice cream machine is broken.**

~ I vow to drink more wine **so I can do something artsy-crafty with the corks.**

~ So, you're one of those people who can actually put the cork back into the wine bottle? **Hahaha, why?**

~ If I ever go missing I want my

picture put on a wine bottle instead of a milk carton. **That way my friends will know I'm missing.**

~ It's that windy outside I've just been blown into this wine bar. **Probably best to stay here until the storm passes.**

~ Who drank all the wine??? **Oh, that's right, it was me, I did it.**

~ Hey, I just met you. And this is crazy. **But here's my wineglass.**

So fill it, maybe?

~ "Mom, where do people
come from?"
"God made us."
Kid, "But Dad said we
come from apes."
**Mom, "He was talking about
his side of the family."**

~ Him: Drink till you want me.
Her: I can't drink that much.

~ An elderly couple are in church and the wife whispers to her husband, "I just did one of those silents farts, what should I do?" **The husband replied, "Well, for a start you can replace the battery in your hearing aid!"**

~My husband asked if he could have a little peace and quiet while he cooked dinner. **So I took the battery out of the smoke alarm.**

~Did you know that 14 muscles are activated when you open a bottle of wine. **Fitness is my passion.**

~Every guy thinks that every girl's dream is to find the perfect guy. **Please, every girl's dream is to eat without getting fat!**

~ Only two things can change a woman's mind.
1. 50% Discount
2. Wine

~ I'm not an alcoholic, alcoholics go to meetings. **I'm a drunk, we go to parties.**

~ My son asked me, "Where does poo come from?" I was a little uncomfortable but gave him an honest explanation. **He looked a little perplexed and stared at me in stunned silence for a few seconds and then asked, "And Tigger?"**

~ Do not let a few glasses of wine serve as an inspiration to call your ex in a pathetic attempt to get back together.

**Some very fine grapes died
in the making of the wine.
Show some respect.**

~ It's Friday night.
**Time to be a hero and rescue
some wine trapped in a bottle.**

~ Sally has a bottle of wine,
there are six glasses of
wine to the bottle.
She drinks three glasses,
what does she have now?
**Happiness.
Sally has happiness.**

People say that drinking milk makes you stronger.

Drink <u>5 glasses of milk</u> and try to move a wall.

Can't?

Now drink <u>5 glasses of wine</u>. The wall moves all by itself!

~ Was at my mom's house helping her clean out her liquor cabinet. She offered me a bottle of vodka they've had for ages. **I had to say no, because I know it's 70% water from me stealing it when I was 16.**

~ For those of you putting Christmas decorations in your garden this year, please avoid red and blue flashing lights. Every time I come round the corner I have to brake hard, toss my phone to the floor and throw my wine out the window, all while trying to drive. **It's too much drama, even for Christmas. Thank you for your cooperation and understanding.**

~ The average person walks 913 miles per year and drinks 556 glasses of wine a year. **Which is 33 miles to the**

gallon, which is pretty good.

~ … and then I said, "Oh, nooo. My glass is empty! **Quick, call wine-one-one."-**

~ It must have been something I ate.

~ If at first you don't succeed...
**Try doing it the way
your wife told you.**

~ Fun fact.
**If you refill a wine glass
before it's empty. it still
counts as one glass.**

~ At the gym: I don't need
an app to tell me how many
calories I've burned.
**I need an app that tells
me how many glasses of
wine I've earned.**

~ The best cure for mid-week blues is wine!

~ If you have to ask if it's too early to drink a glass of wine. **You're an amateur and we can't be friends.**

~ A good man can make you feel sexy, strong and able to take on the world. **Oh, wait. Sorry, that's wine, wine does that.**

~ How do two cats end a fight? They hiss
and make up!

~ If anyone tells you it's too early
to drink... unfriend them.
**You don't need that kind of
negativity in your life!**

~ **First aid for wine.**

1.Pour a glass to allow it to breathe.
2. If it doesn't look like it's breathing give it mouth to mouth.

~ Every box of raisins is a tragic tale of grapes **that could have been wine.**

~ Anyone who doesn't know what to buy me for Christmas, **clearly doesn't know where to buy wine.**

A rabbit eats vegetables, runs and hops all day long, and lives 5 years.

Meanwhile a tortoise doesn't run, doesn't hop and does nothing energetic, yet it can live 200 years.

And you tell me I need to eat well and exercise!

I don't think so.

~ I love romantic walks…
**to the kitchen to get
a glass of wine.**

~ I ate a kid's Meal at
McDonalds this morning.
His mother was furious.

~ There are only two types
of people in this world,
those who like wine
**and those who aren't
allowed in my house.**

~ I love cooking with wine.

Sometimes I even put some in the food.

~ Great minds drink alike.

~ Don't ask me why I love wine, **I have my Rieslings.**

Post-Coronavirus males, displaying their Hunter Gatherer prowess in order to attract mates

~ Today's forecast:
**Partly cloudy with a
100% chance of wine.**

~ Just another Merlot Monday.

~ Another wine bottle
drank and emptied with no
genie in the bottom?
Then I'll keep trying.

~ I hear you like wine too?
Grape minds think alike.

~ Love the wine you're with.

~ My favorite exercise at
the gym is a cross between
a lunge and a crunch.
I call it 'lunch.'

~ Another glass?
Wine not.

~ Wine improves with age.
I improve with wine.

~ Am feeling great,
I must be on cloud wine.

Another glass of this delicious liquid? Wine-derful!

~ Meals served without wine are **rarely worth eating.**

~ It doesn't matter if the glass is half empty or half full. **There's room for more wine.**

~ I put my bathroom scale in the corner and that's where the little liar will stay until she apologises.

~ You had me at Merlot.

I keep two glasses of wine ready. **One for me and one for when I forget where I left the other one.**

~ Okay, I admit I did have a little to drink today, but I saw two guys wearing matching outfits and I asked them if they were gay.

They arrested me.

I used to be stressed out a lot, but then I discovered Yoga. I'm feeling so much better now.

~ Bankteller: Your account is overdrawn.

Me: Well, so are your
eyebrows, but here we are.

~ You're how old? Poor
you! I mean,
pour you another glass of wine.

~ Somehow they knew I
wanted champagne.
It was chilling.

~ How Merlot can you go.

When your Dad helps you dress up for Halloween :)

~ It's going to be a wine-derful day.

~ Happiness is a well-stocked wine cabinet **and a closet full of shoes.**

~ I have joy in my heart and a glass of wine in my hand. **Coincidence?? I don't think so.**

~ Come to drink of it, **we're going to need more wine.**

~ This guy once told me, "You're never going to forget me." **Wise words - I just wish I could remember who the hell it was.**

~ What's a girl's idea of
a balanced diet?
A glass of wine in each hand.

~ At Christmas time there's
nothing I love more than
sitting in front of a warm
fire, mulled wine in hand
and singing Christmas songs
until I slowly fall asleep.
**Maybe I should stop
being a fireman?**

~ **I'm great at multi-tasking.
I can listen, ignore and forget**

all at the same time.

~ You're so vine you probably think this wine is about you.

Looks like Santa got my list!

~ Let's get fizz-ical
with some Champagne.

~ Drink wine -
**You can't regret what
you don't remember.**

~ You and me.
Partners in wine.

~ Wine flies when
you're having fun.

~ When I drink wine **I make pour decisions.**

~ My friend asked if I was happy. **I told her I was on cloud wine.**

~ A baby-shower game requested everyone write parenting advice on a notecard. **I wrote down my favorite margarita recipe.**

~ I'm feeling wine and dandy.

~ I have joy in my heart

and a glass of wine in my hand. **Coincidence??**

"I love you," I said, quietly.

My husband asked, "is that you or the wine talking?"

I replied, "it's me talking to my wine."

~ If asked if I'd rather be rich, famous, or a good mom, I'd say two out of those three would be nice. **I mean, it would be no fun to be famous but poor.**

~Did you know drinking 2 to 3 glasses of wine a day reduces your risk of giving a damn?

~ I hear you also like a glass of wine. **Grape minds think alike.**

~ I'm not old.
I'm aged to perfection
and full-bodied.

I decided to make sure
my husband woke up
with a big smile on his
face this morning.

Now I can't have
Sharpies in the house
anymore.

~ He said his non-alcoholic

wine was delicious,
I said he had no proof.

~ New Years Resolution:
This coming year no alcohol
will touch my lips!
I'm going to use a straw.

~ They say being nice to other
people's kids won't kill you.
**But, honestly, I'd rather
not risk it.**

~ Wine is like duck tape,
it fixes everything.

~ I only drink wine on days that end with a 'Y.'

~ A meal without wine **is called breakfast.**

~ I've been happier since I changed from coffee in the morning to orange juice. **My doctor explained that it's the vitamin C but I really think it's the Vodka.**

~ I've trained my dog to

bring me a glass of red wine.
It's a Bordeaux collie.

~ "Somebody stole my cycle," said the priest to his friend. "What do you think I should do?"
"Why don't use the 10 Commandments, in your sermon this Sunday," replied the friend "And when you get to the part about stealing, stress the words, 'Thou Shalt Not Steal.' Then pause and look out to the congregation and see if anyone looks guilty or shuffles in their seat."

"Good idea, I'll do it," responds the priest.

So, that Sunday the friend sits in the congregation and listens. The priest does his sermon and goes through the 10 Commandments but doesn't stress any part of it, or pause to watch for a reaction. Afterwards, the friend asks the priest why he didn't do as he had suggested.

"Well," says the priest. "I started and all was going well, but then I got to the commandment, **'Thou shalt not Commit Adultery,"** he continued. **"And I remembered where I'd left my pedal-bike."**

~ I have an open-door policy.
**Show up with wine and
I'll open the door.**

~ What do you call a
wine hangover?
The grape depression.

~ Wine improves with age.
I improve with wine.

Wine Puns

1. Great minds drink alike.

2. I make pour decisions.

3. Here for the right Reislings.

4. On cloud wine.

5. Partners in wine.

6. No wine left behind.

7. Sip happens.

8. It's wine o'clock.

9. Stop and smell the rosé

10. Everything happens
for a riesling, right?

11. Love the wine you're with.

12. Oh, sweet child of wine.

13. I need to re-wine my life.

14. You're the wine that I want.

15. You are so bottlefull to me.

16. I decide which wine to drink on a case by case basis.

17. She only made gin, but he loved her still.

18. Grape minds think alike.

19. Where there's a wine there's a way.

20. Yes way, Rosé!

Me: I think I'm a moth.
Doctor: You need to see a psychiatrist for that.
Me: I know.
Doctor: Then why are you here?
Me: The light was on.

21. Happy hour? Wine not?

22. Back that glass up.

23. Just a sip to help me un-wine.

24. Great minds drink alike.

25. Now you just wait
a Prosecco-nd.

26. Do I like wine? You bet Shiraz I do!

27. If you can't be with the one you love, love the wine you're with.

28. Say you'll be wine.

29. I'm feeling vine and dandy.

30. Sip, sip, hooray!

I was mortified when I caught my husband dressed up in my clothes.

That skirt with those shoes?

I don't think so!

~ Don't ask me why I love wine.
I have my rieslings.

~ A friend once said,
"Sometimes you have to hug
the people you don't like
**just so you know how big to
dig the hole in the backyard."**

~ Tomorrow is National
Stay at Home with Your Pet
and Drink Wine Day.
**It's nothing official, I made
it up, but tell your friends!**

~ Women know, they just know!
Even if they didn't know,
they'd still know.

Men probably won't get this, but women will... because they know.

~ I'm trying to eat more fruit so I ate a big bag of grapes last night. Well, when I say bag, I mean bottle, **and when I say ate, I mean drank.**

~ Cop, 'Please step out of the car, Madam.'

Me, 'I'm too drunk, you get in.'

Does the jelly in a donut count as a serving of fruit? **Asking for a friend.**

~ Today's forecast partly cloudy with 100% chance of wine.

~And now, a drum roll please, our last joke.

~ My friend asked: What's in the bag? Me: A bottle of wine, I got it for my husband. **Friend: Good trade!**

We hope you have laughed and enjoyed our **A Very Necessary Wine Joke Book.** *If you have, please tell your friends and others about it.*

If you are looking for a present for a dad or a husband, take a look at our **Totally Awesome Dad Joke Book** *on Amazon. I know you will enjoy it.*

And please leave us positive feedback with Amazon and perhaps a high star rating.... It is important to us and we would greatly appreciate it.

Thank you! Zack Halliday

Made in United States
North Haven, CT
22 September 2022

24430203R00061